Beyond the Surface

(A Jesusbride Collection)

Dedication

This book is dedicated to my Father, Dr. Tolulope Akinbode Oyetayo. A relentless, hardworking, principled, caring, and God-fearing man

On a cold winter night, after a long, busy day, Bukky fell into a deep sleep. In a dream, he found himself on top of water in the middle of a sea. To his side, he could see the side view of a black man clothed in white apparel. This unfamiliar person was to be his guide on this adventure.

It was busy at sea; many different people came for different purposes. They all had their unique equipments with them to help them stay afloat. Bukky noticed a group of young boisterous people surfing. He could hear one of them saying amusingly and affirmatively to herself, "Jesus walked on water, and we are also doing the same."

Then, in another view and to his amazement, Bukky was shown a meandering path on the sea. He never for once in his entire life imagined that such pathways could exist on water bodies in reality.

Looking farther ahead, he observed that the path those youngsters were surfing was fusing into the meandering path. At this time, he could see that the meandering pathway was headed to a sink hole, a pit-like funnel in the sea, and the youngsters were only a few metres away from it.

Bukky continued to watch the scene closely and in eagerness to learn what was about to happen. For some reason, a young lady called 'Becky' mysteriously came into Bukky's focus.

She was then quite close to the mouth of the sinkhole. Some of her friends were already being engulfed by the sink hole.

It was at that time point, that the tour guide first spoke. He said to Becky in an authoritative voice,

GET OUT OF THERE, COME OUT OF THOSE PLACES OF UNCERTAINTY !!!

Bukky was awestruck.

Becky's surfboard was miraculously shifted off the meandering path, then she began to drift closer till she reached Bukky's vessel. Bukky's vessel had been anchored to the rock all along while the tour guide kept him company.

An enchanting voice started calling out around the depression zone, 'Don't be in such a rush to figure everything out, Embrace the unknown and let your life surprise you.'

There was lightning, fireworks and storm-like displays around the hole, but it was too late for Becky to return because she was already rescued.

Becky was completely unaware that she was heading to destruction as she was a confident, trained and qualified sea surfer.

Becky accompanied Bukky and the tour guide to the shore. The onlooking crowd kept cheering, 'Jesus is Wicked, even the winds obey him !'

Bukky woke up from his dream thinking:

No matter how much in control we seem to be, are we in right-standing with God?

Have we pondered where we are headed? I am waking up to rightful living.

Then he began to remember scriptures from the Bible.

There is a way which seemed right unto a man, but the end thereof are the ways of death.

Prov. 14 vs 12 KJV

When thou pssest through the waters, I will be with thee; and through the rivers, they shall not overflow thee: when thou walkest through the fire, thou shalt not be burned; neither shall the flame kindle upon thee.

Isaiah 43 vs 2 KJV

And Jesus said unto him, Why callest thou me good? there is none good but one, that is, God.

Mark 10 vs 18 KJV

The End

Your Thoughts

_____

_____

_____

_____

_____

_____

_____

_____

_____

Do you want to share your thoughts with the authors? or provide feedback? Please complete the response form via the link:

https://forms.gle/fsKXp2YW446GzXHQA

or scan the QR code below:

Beyond the Surface
Author: Olubukayo Oladunjoye
Illustration: Ayomide Adeeko
Graphics design: Tolulope Folorunso

www.ingramcontent.com/pod-product-compliance
Lightning Source LLC
Chambersburg PA
CBHW041446120626
46547CB00002B/370